SCOTTISH MEAT RECIPES

Some hae meat and canna eat,
  And some would eat that want it;
But we hae meat, and we can eat,
  Sae let the Lord be thankit.

Robert Burns

Index

Cover pictures *front:* 'Highland Cattle' *by John Wright Barker RBA*
back: 'On the High Tops' *by Archibald Thorburn*
Title page: 'Monarch of the Glen' *by Sir Edwin Landseer RA*
Printed and Published by J. Salmon Ltd., Sevenoaks, England

Aberdeen Angus Beef Olives

Olives have featured in cooking since the 1600's and Aberdeen Angus beef gives a superb flavour.

1½ lbs topside Aberdeen Angus beef   4 rashers streaky bacon
3 onions, thinly sliced   4 oz fresh breadcrumbs   4 oz shredded beef suet
2 teaspoons chopped fresh parsley   ½ teaspoon dried mixed herbs
1 lemon   1 egg, beaten   1 tablespoon made English mustard
3 oz seasoned flour   1 oz butter   2 tablespoons vegetable oil
15 fl.oz beef stock   Salt and pepper

Set oven to 325°F or Mark 3. Finely chop the bacon and one of the onions and mix with the breadcrumbs, suet, parsley, herbs, grated zest of half the lemon, 1 teaspoon of the lemon juice and the beaten egg. Cut the meat into 8 thin slices and beat out flat with a mallet or rolling pin. Thinly spread mustard over each piece, together with the stuffing mixture, equally divided. Roll up the meat and secure each 'olive' with butcher's string. Dust each 'olive' with seasoned flour. Heat the butter and oil in a shallow, heavybottom casserole dish and fry the 'olives' until browned all over. Remove the 'olives' from the pan and set aside. Stir the remaining flour into the meat juices, then add the stock gradually and bring to the boil, stirring frequently. Return the 'olives' to the casserole, cover with the 2 remaining sliced onions, season, cover and cook for about 1½ hours. Remove the string before serving. Serves 4 to 6.

'A Highland Family' *by Henry William Banks Davis*

Mince and Tatties

This variation on the plain Mince and Tatties recipe is full of extra vegetables; children will never notice! In Scotland the vegetable 'swede' is known as 'turnip'.

1 lb best minced beef
1 medium onion
1 medium carrot
2 oz turnip (swede)
1 tablespoon vegetable oil
2 teaspoons Bovril
1 teaspoon redcurrant jelly
1 teaspoon tomato purée
1 tablespoon mushroom ketchup
1 stick of celery, left whole
Salt and pepper

Cut the onion, carrot and turnip (swede) into chunks and blitz in a food processor until finely chopped. Alternatively they can be well grated by hand. Heat the oil in a saucepan, add the mince and cook for 3 to 4 minutes. Add the finely chopped vegetables and cook for a further 2 to 3 minutes. Add all the other ingredients, including the stick of celery, season and cover with water. Bring up to heat, cover and simmer for 40 to 45 minutes. When cooked, remove the celery stick. Serve with buttery mashed potato. Serves 4.

Venison Patties

A tasty dish with a piquant sauce and a way to use up left-over cooked venison.

1 lb cooked venison meat, minced
1 small onion, very finely chopped or minced
Salt and pepper Butter for frying
½ pint white sauce 1 tablespoon French mustard
1 teaspoon sugar Dash of Worcestershire sauce
1 teaspoon horseradish sauce (if desired)

Set oven to 375°F or Mark 5. Mix the minced venison and onion and season well. Form the mixture into round patties about 1 to 1½ inches in diameter. Fry the patties gently in butter until brown on both sides and then transfer to a small casserole dish. Prepare the white sauce and stir in the mustard, sugar and Worcestershire sauce (a teaspoon of horseradish sauce can also be added to give the sauce more bite). Pour the mixture over the patties and bake for 30 minutes. Serves 4.

Highland Bake

A baked dish of oatmeal, vegetables and bacon, topped with pork sausages.

1 lb pork sausages
8 oz back bacon rashers
1 oz lard for frying
4 oz chopped onions
4 oz tomatoes, skinned and chopped
2 oz fresh breadcrumbs
1 oz medium oatmeal
Salt and pepper
1 egg
2 tablespoons milk

Set oven to 350°F or Mark 4. De-rind the bacon, chop it into small pieces and fry, in the lard, over a low heat, with the onions. Blanch the tomatoes in boiling water, remove the skins and chop the flesh. Add the chopped tomatoes and cook for a further 2 minutes. Transfer the mixture from the pan to a bowl and stir in the breadcrumbs and oatmeal. Season well. Beat together the egg and milk and mix in. Spoon the mixture into a shallow, ovenproof dish and arrange the sausages on top. Bake for about 30 minutes or until the sausages are cooked. Serves 4.

Scotch Broth

Meat, barley and vegetables are the essential ingredients for this warming soup.

1 lb neck of mutton or lamb
2½ pints water
1 oz pearl barley
Salt and pepper
1 small white turnip, chopped
1 leek, chopped
1 large carrot, chopped
1 onion, chopped
1 small carrot, grated
1 oz cabbage, shredded
Chopped parsley to garnish

Put the meat in a saucepan with the water. Add the pearl barley and season with salt and pepper. Bring to the boil, cover and simmer for 1 hour. Skim off any white scum. Add the chopped vegetables, cover and simmer for another 1 hour, adding the grated carrot and the cabbage for the final 30 minutes of cooking. Before serving, remove the meat and bones and discard the bones. The meat can be returned to the broth or eaten separately, if preferred. Bring back to the boil and serve, garnished with chopped parsley. Serves 4 to 6.

'A West Highland Group' *by William Watson*

Rich Pork Hotpot

The whisky, apple juice and mustard combine beautifully to create this rich casserole.

1 lb pork fillet, cubed
2 oz butter
1 large onion, sliced
8 oz mushrooms, sliced
2 tablespoons flour
5 fl. oz beef or chicken stock
5 fl. oz whisky
5 fl. oz apple juice
1 tablespoon French mustard
Salt & pepper

Melt the butter in a pan and brown the meat. Add the onion and mushrooms and cook for 2 to 3 minutes. Stir in the flour and cook for a further 2 minutes. Add the stock, whisky, apple juice and mustard, stir and bring to the boil. Cover and simmer for 40 minutes. Season to taste. Serve with creamy mashed potato. Serves 4.

Potted Hough

Hough is the Scottish word for shin. This traditional paste is ideal for sandwiches, picnics or on toast as a starter.

2 lb shin of beef, meat on the bone and the bone cracked
Pinch of ground allspice
Pinch of cayenne pepper
Salt and pepper

Put the meat into a large pan with the allspice and cayenne pepper. Cover with cold water and bring to the boil. Turn down the heat to a very low simmer and cook for at least 6 hours, skimming occasionally. When cooked, remove the meat, strain the liquid and allow it to cool. Skim off the fat. Separate the meat from the bone, mince it and return to the stock. Season with salt and pepper to taste and simmer for another 15 minutes. Wet some small moulds or ramekins and divide the mixture between them. Allow to cool slightly and then place in the refrigerator to set. When set, turn out and serve on buttered toast or in sandwiches.

'Highland Cattle with Sheep' *by Charles Jones RCA*

Beef with Blue Cheese

Beef and blue cheese make the perfect combination.
Ideally use one of the Scottish blues.

4 lean beef steaks
2 tablespoons vegetable oil
1 red onion, thinly sliced
4 oz blue cheese
4 tablespoons soft cream cheese
2 tablespoons milk
2 teaspoons made English mustard

Heat the oil in a pan and fry the steaks to the desired degree. Remove from the pan, transfer to a serving dish and keep hot. Fry the sliced red onion until soft but not brown. Stir in the cheeses, milk and mustard and cook gently until thoroughly melted and heated through. Serve the steaks with the sauce poured over, together with new potatoes and seasonal vegetables. Serves 4.

Stoved Chicken

'Stoved' dishes were so called because they were cooked on top of the range or stove rather than in the oven.

4 small chicken breasts, skinned and sliced thinly
2 oz butter
2 lb old potatoes, peeled and sliced about ¼ inch thick
Salt and pepper 2 large onions, sliced
1 pint chicken stock 2 tablespoons chopped parsley

Melt 1 oz of the butter in a large heavy bottom saucepan or flameproof casserole and lightly brown the chicken slices. Remove from the pan and set aside. To assemble the dish in the pan or casserole, start with a thick layer of potatoes. Season, then add a layer of onion followed by a layer of chicken. Repeat until all have been used, finishing with a layer of potatoes. Pour over the stock. Dot with small knobs of the remaining butter, bring up to heat, cover and simmer slowly for about 2 hours. Top up with a little water if it appears to be drying out too quickly. Sprinkle with parsley before serving. Serves 4.

Inky-Pinky

Never waste a morsel – this economical dish uses left-overs from a typical Sunday lunch.

Cold roast beef, sliced
½ pint left-over gravy (or good beef stock made from bones)
Left-over carrots or other root vegetables
1 onion, sliced
1 teaspoon redcurrant jelly
Red wine vinegar, to taste

Put all the ingredients into a large saucepan, cover and simmer slowly over a low heat until thoroughly heated through and the onion is softened. Add a dash of red wine vinegar to taste. Serve with mashed potato. Serves 4.

Grouse Casserole

A good way of casseroling slightly older grouse, with the added flavour of whisky.

Brace of grouse, trussed
3 oz butter
1 onion, chopped
4 oz mushrooms, chopped
1 stick of celery, diced
2 carrots, diced
2 tablespoons whisky
10 fl.oz chicken stock
1 tablespoon redcurrant jelly

Set oven to 350°F or Mark 4. Heat the butter in a heavy casserole dish and brown the grouse all over. Remove from the pan and set aside. Add the chopped and diced vegetables to the pan and cook gently until soft but not browned. Return the grouse to the pan and add the whisky. Flame the spirit and when the flames have disappeared add the stock. Bring up to heat, cover and cook for about 1¼ hours. When cooked, remove the grouse and, using shears, cut each bird in half, set aside on a large serving dish and keep hot. Strain the liquid into a saucepan and boil. When it starts to thicken add the redcurrant jelly, allow it to dissolve and then spoon over the grouse with the strained vegetables. Serves 4.

'Red and Black Grouse Feeding' *by Archibald Thorburn*

Beef Dumplings

Also called Highland Beef Balls, these fried dumplings are best served with mashed potato.

1 lb best beef mince   6 oz shredded beef suet
1½ oz onions, finely chopped   Salt and pepper
¼ teaspoon each, ground cloves, ginger and mace
1 egg, lightly beaten   Medium oatmeal for coating
Lard for frying

In a bowl, mix the mince with the suet and chopped onions. Season well and add the spices. Lightly beat the egg and combine with the meat mixture. Shape the mixture into 2 inch balls and roll in the oatmeal. Deep fry in lard until brown (approx 8 to 10 minutes). Serve with a fresh tomato sauce. Serves 4.

Devilled Kidneys

A traditional and delicious breakfast dish..

12 lamb kidneys
Flour seasoned with cayenne pepper, mustard powder, salt and pepper
Cooking oil and butter for frying
Knob of butter   Worcestershire sauce
4 slices of white toast

Split each kidney in half and remove white core. Mix sufficient flour with cayenne pepper, mustard powder, salt and pepper and dust the kidney halves in the mixture. Heat the oil and butter in a heavy bottom frying pan until very hot. Fry the kidneys for 2 to 3 minutes each side and arrange on the prepared slices of toast. Add a knob of butter to the pan with a good sprinkling of Worcestershire sauce, stir and mix with the juices over the heat. Pour the hot mixture over the kidneys and toast. Serves 4.

'A Highland Flock' *by Robert Watson*

Tattie Pot

Also known as mutton and potato pie, this is a hot-pot from the Borders.

4 lamb chops, middle neck
2 lamb kidneys, cored
1 lb potatoes, peeled and sliced
1 small black pudding, sliced
3 oz onions, sliced
5 oz carrots, sliced
Salt and pepper
5 fl.oz white stock
½ oz lard, melted

Set oven to 350°F or Mark 4. Slice the kidneys, remove the white cores and fry with the lamb chops in their own fat over a high heat for 3 minutes. Place a layer of potatoes in an ovenproof dish, then cover with half the chops, kidneys and black pudding, onions and carrots. Season and cover with more potatoes. Repeat with all the remaining ingredients, finishing with a layer of potatoes. Pour over the stock and brush the potatoes with melted lard. Bring up to heat, cover and cook in the oven for 1½ to 2 hours. Remove the lid, increase the oven temperature to 425°F or Mark 7 and cook for a further 30 minutes. Serves 4.

Kingdom of Fife Pie

A traditional rabbit pie with forcemeat stuffing balls.

1 rabbit, jointed
8 oz bacon, cubed
2 hard-boiled eggs, quartered
3 oz breadcrumbs
1 oz bacon fat, chopped
Pinch of dried thyme
Salt and pepper
1 egg, beaten
10 fl.oz chicken stock
1 lb shortcrust pastry

Set oven to 425°F or Mark 7. Joint the rabbit and set aside the liver. Hard boil 2 eggs. Arrange the rabbit joints, bacon (use either bacon pieces or coarsely chopped rashers) and hard-boiled eggs in a pie dish. Finely chop the rabbit liver and mix with the breadcrumbs, bacon fat and thyme. Season and bind the mixture with the beaten egg. Divide into about 8 stuffing balls and place into the pie. Add the stock. Roll out the pastry on a floured surface and cover the pie. Trim, make a steam hole and glaze. Bake for 15 minutes then reduce the oven temperature to 350°F or Mark 4 and continue baking for a further 1 to 1¼ hours until golden brown. Serves 4

Bacon Stovies

A simple way of preparing bacon on top of the stove.

2-2½ lb of forehock bacon
2 lb potatoes, peeled and sliced
1 lb onions, chopped
Mustard powder
Black pepper
1 bayleaf
Milk as required

Cut the bacon into 1 inch cubes. In a heavy saucepan or casserole dish, place alternate layers of bacon, potatoes and onions, sprinkling each layer with a little mustard powder and pepper. Finish with a layer of potatoes. Add the bayleaf and sufficient milk to come level with the top layer of potatoes. Bring to a low boil, cover and simmer gently for 1½ to 2 hours. Serves 6 to 8.

Whisky Stroganoff

A Scottish variation of the classic beef dish.

12 oz fillet steak (or good rump)
4 oz butter
1 large onion, finely sliced
8 oz mushrooms, sliced
2 tablespoons whisky
5 fl. oz double cream
Salt and pepper

Cut the steak into ½ inch slices and pound with a mallet or rolling pin until very thin. Cut into strips about 1 inch in length. Melt half the butter in a frying pan and fry the onions gently until just browned. Add the mushrooms and cook for a further 2 minutes. Remove the onions and mushrooms from the pan and set aside. Add the remaining butter to the pan, heat well and quickly fry the steak strips until brown. Return the onions and mushrooms to the pan, add the whisky and cream and season to taste. Stir well to incorporate the pan juices and re-heat gently until thoroughly heated through, but do not allow to boil. Serve with plain boiled rice or noodles. Serves 4.

'Highland Cattle' *by William Watson*

Devilled Game

A quick and easy recipe to give game a delicious flavour.

4 joints of game (or poultry)

PASTE
4 oz butter, softened
2 tablespoons mango chutney
1 tablespoon Worcestershire sauce
1 tablespoon Dijon mustard
1 teaspoon curry powder (to choice)
2 drops Tabasco sauce

Preheat the grill to a moderate heat. Make the paste by mixing all the ingredients together into a buttery paste. With a very sharp knife, make slashes in the skin and flesh of the game joints. Spread the paste generously over the joints and work into the flesh. Put the joints on the grill pan and grill for about 10 to 15 minutes on each side, basting with the sauce that drips into the pan. Finally, test with a skewer to ensure the meat is cooked through. Serve with the sauce poured over the joints. Serves 4.

Mutton Pies

Excellent hot or cold, these simple pies are typically Scottish.

FILLING

12 oz lean mutton or lamb   Salt and pepper
6 tablespoons meat stock, gravy or water

HOT WATER CRUST

8 oz flour   Pinch salt   2 oz lard or vegetable fat
2 fl.oz water   2 fl.oz milk   1 egg yolk for glazing

Make the filling first. Chop the meat finely and season. Set aside. Set oven to 375°F or Mark 5. Make the hot water crust. Sieve the flour and salt into a bowl. Boil the lard, water and milk together in a saucepan. Make a well in the flour and pour in the hot mixture: mix well with a knife and knead until smooth. Roll out two thirds of the pastry on a floured surface, keeping a third for lids. Cut into 6 circles and press into deep patty tins. Spoon the meat into each tin, moistening each filling with a spoonful of stock, gravy or water. Cut the remaining dough into 6 smaller circles for lids. Brush the edges with water and seal. Make a slit in each pie lid to allow steam to escape. Brush with egg yolk. Cook in the oven for 30 to 40 minutes. Serve hot or cold. As a variation, add some chopped onion, mushroom and parsley to the filling.

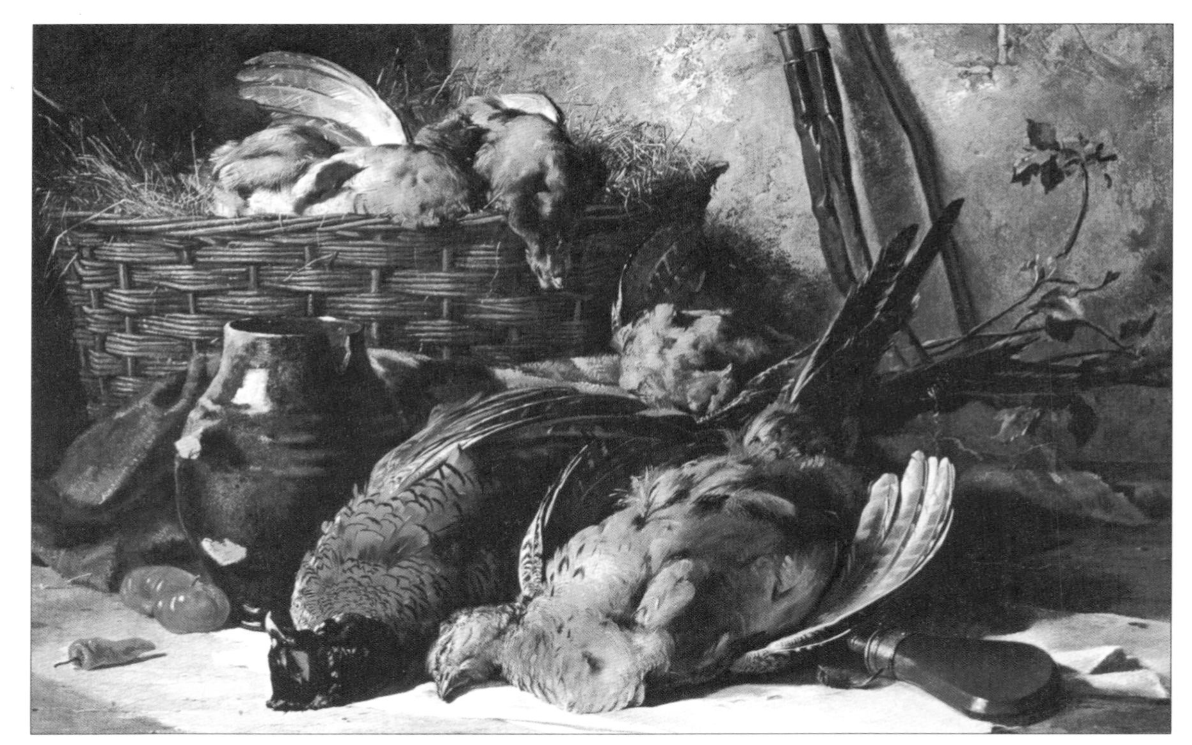

'A Brace of Pheasants' *by James Hardy Jnr.*

Braised Pheasant with Whisky

The whisky adds a Scottish flavour to this dish.

Brace of pheasants, jointed
8 rashers streaky bacon
8 fresh bay leaves
3 fl.oz vegetable oil
8 oz shallots, peeled and left whole
6 fl.oz whisky
10 fl.oz chicken stock
A bouquet garni
Salt and pepper

Joint each pheasant into 4 pieces (the butcher can do this, if required). Wrap each joint with a bacon rasher, secure with a cocktail stick and tuck 1 bay leaf under the bacon wrapper. Heat the oil in a large heavy bottom pan and fry the pheasant joints until brown on both sides. Remove the joints and keep warm. Add the shallots to the pan and gently cook until softened, turning so that they are sautéed all over. Remove and set aside. Add the whisky and then the stock to the pan and bring to the boil, stirring continuously. Boil for 5 minutes, stirring. Add the *bouquet garni* and season well. Return the pheasant joints and the shallots to the pan, reduce the heat and simmer gently for 45 minutes. Remove the cocktail sticks before serving. Serves 4 to 6.

Farmer's Brew

A delicious stew which is cooked in beer.

1½ lb stewing steak
1 oz seasoned flour
2 oz butter
4 oz onions, sliced
1 oz granulated sugar
Pinch of mustard powder
Sprig of fresh thyme
1 bayleaf
Salt and pepper
10 fl.oz Scottish ale
5 fl.oz beef stock

Set oven to 400°F or Mark 6. Slice the meat into thin strips and toss in the seasoned flour. Melt the butter in a heavy ovenproof casserole dish and brown the meat and onions. Add the sugar, mustard, thyme and bayleaf and season well. Bring up to heat, cover and cook in the oven for 10 minutes. Remove from the oven, add the beer and stock and bring to the boil. Reduce the oven temperature to 325°F or Mark 3. Return the casserole to the oven and cook for a further 1½ hours. Serve on a bed of mashed potato. Serves 4 to 6.

Curried Chicken Soup

A sweet and spicy version of chicken soup.

1 oz butter 1 stick celery, chopped 1 onion, chopped
2 medium carrots, sliced 1 dessert apple, peeled, cored & quartered
½ teaspoon curry powder 4 oz left-over cooked chicken pieces
1½ pints chicken stock Salt & pepper
1 teaspoon chopped fresh coriander 4 tablespoons cream or plain yoghurt

Melt the butter in a saucepan and add the celery, onion and carrots. Cover and sweat for 5 minutes. Add the apple slices, curry powder and cooked chicken and pour in the stock. Cover and simmer for 40 minutes. Remove from the heat and allow to cool a little. Transfer to a food processor and blend until smooth. Return the soup to the pan, season to taste and bring back up to heat. Serve garnished with chopped fresh coriander and add a tablespoon of cream or yoghurt to each bowl. Serves 4.

Venison Pie

The combination of venison, red wine and redcurrant jelly makes for a delicious and rich pie.

2 lb venison shoulder
2 oz flour
Pinch ground mace
Pinch of all-spice
Salt and pepper
5 fl.oz red wine
5 fl.oz red wine vinegar
10 fl.oz venison stock
2 onions, sliced
½ tablespoon chopped fresh parsley
1 tablespoon redcurrant jelly
12 oz puff pastry

Set oven to 450°F or Mark 8. First tenderise the meat with a mallet or rolling pin and remove any fat and gristle. Mix the flour, mace and all-spice and season well. Cube the meat and dust with the flour mixture. Put in a pan with the wine, vinegar and sufficient stock to cover the meat. Simmer gently for 1 hour, then add the onions and parsley. Cover and simmer for another 30 minutes. Remove from the heat, allow to cool and skim off any fat from the surface. Put the meat mixture in a pie dish, add the redcurrant jelly and the remaining stock. Roll out the pastry on a floured surface, cover the pie, seal the edges, make a steam hole and bake for about 25 minutes until the pastry is golden brown. Serves 4 to 6.

'Defiance' *by W. H. Dyer*

Pickled Beef

A Scottish way of cooking stewing steak – the marinade tenderises the meat.

2 lb stewing steak
3 fl.oz olive oil
3 fl.oz red wine vinegar
6 cloves
12 black peppercorns
Fresh thyme and parsley
12 oz onions, sliced
2 bayleaves
2 oz butter
3 fl.oz beef stock
Salt and pepper

Cut the meat into 6 to 8 pieces. Prepare the marinade by mixing the oil, vinegar, cloves and peppercorns with a sprig each of thyme and parsley. Lay the meat in a dish with the onions and bayleaves and cover with the marinade. Cover the dish and leave to steep overnight Next day, drain the meat and pat dry. Heat the butter in a pan and fry the meat on both sides to the preferred degree. Remove from the pan, set aside on a warm serving dish and keep hot. Add the stock and about 3 to 4 tablespoons of the marinade to the butter and meat juices in the pan and boil quickly to reduce. Season to taste and pour over the beef. Serves 6 to 8.

Wild Duck in Cream Sauce

This dish is not for those who are counting the calories!

2 ducks, prepared for the oven
1 medium onion, finely chopped
1½ pints double cream
2 tablespoons redcurrant jelly
1 oz Scottish blue cheese, crumbled
Juice of 1 lemon
2 tablespoons rowan jelly
Salt & pepper

Set oven to 425°F – 450°F or Mark 7-8. Roast the ducks on a rack for about 30 minutes until the skin is crisp and brown and much of the fat has run out (gently prick the skin with a skewer to release excess fat). Drain the ducks well and put in a large casserole dish with the chopped onion. Add the cream and redcurrant jelly. Cover and cook for about 1 to 1½ hours until the ducks are tender (test each leg with a skewer to ensure the ducks are cooked through). Lift the ducks out of the casserole, set aside on a dish and keep hot. Skim the fat from the sauce, return the casserole to the stove and and boil quickly to reduce the sauce by one third. Then, stir in the cheese, lemon juice and rowan jelly, mix well and season to taste. Serve with new potatoes and green vegetables. Serves 4 to 6.

'Suspicion' *by Joseph Devonan Adam RSA*

Beef in Red Wine

Historically there have been strong links between Scotland and France, so French red wine, especially claret, was widely used.

1½ lb stewing steak, cubed
1 tablespoon seasoned flour
2 oz lean bacon, chopped
3 small onions, sliced
7 oz button mushrooms, chopped
2 tablespoons vegetable oil
2 cloves of garlic, crushed
½ bottle red wine
½ teaspoon sugar
A bouquet garni
Salt and pepper

Set oven to 300°F or Mark 2. Gently fry the bacon and then add the onions and cook until soft. Add the mushrooms and fry for a few minutes. Set the mixture aside and keep warm. Cut the steak into 1½ inch cubes and dust with seasoned flour. Heat the oil in a heavy bottom casserole dish and fry the meat and garlic until brown. Add the wine, sugar and *bouquet garni* and season. Stir well, bring up to heat, cover and cook for about 2 hours or until the meat is tender. Remove from the oven and stir in the bacon mixture. Heat for a further 5 to 10 minutes and serve with boiled or mashed potatoes. Serves 4 to 6.

Cream of Kidney Soup

The richness and sweetness of lambs' kidneys in a delicious soup.

4 lamb kidneys, cored and finely chopped   1 oz butter
1 large onion, finely diced   1 tablespoon flour
¾ pint beef stock (or made with 3 teaspoons Bovril)
Salt and pepper   ¼ pint milk   ¼ pint single cream
2 tablespoons whisky
1 teaspoon fresh finely chopped chives

Melt the butter in a saucepan and add the chopped kidneys and onion. Cook for 2 to 3 minutes then stir in the flour. Add the stock, season to taste, cover and simmer gently for 20 minutes. Remove from the heat and stir in the milk, cream and whisky. Bring back up to heat but do not boil. Serve garnished with a small sprinkling of chopped chives. Serves 4.

Forfar Bridies

These small steak pies originated in Forfar, one story being that they were invented by Margaret Bridie of Glamis, another that they were prepared as simple dishes for wedding meals (i.e. Bridies).

12 oz best stewing steak
1 medium onion, chopped finely
Salt and pepper
¼ teaspoon mustard powder
3 oz shredded beef suet
1 lb shortcrust pastry
Beaten egg to glaze

Set oven to 350°F or Mark 4. Chop the meat into very small pieces or mince coarsely. Put in a bowl with the chopped onion, salt, pepper and mustard. Sprinkle on the suet and mix well. Cut the pastry into 3 pieces and roll out each piece on a floured surface to a round about ¼ inch thick. Spoon the meat on to one half of each round, taking care not to overfill. Dampen the edges of the pastry, fold to make semi-circles and pinch the edges together to resemble small Cornish pasties. Place on a plain baking sheet. Brush with beaten egg and make a hole in each one for the steam to escape. Bake for about 1¼ hours until golden brown; if the pastry is browning too quickly, cover with kitchen foil. Serve hot with vegetables or cold as a snack. Makes 3 pasties.

Curried Lamb Shanks

Curries of all kinds are a favourite throughout Scotland.

4 lamb shanks (3½ to 4 lb total weight)   1 tablespoon vegetable oil
3 cloves garlic, peeled & crushed roughly
1 inch piece fresh root ginger, peeled & grated
2 onions, chopped   1 oz flour   Juice and rind of 1 orange
5 fl.oz white wine   2 tablespoons rice vinegar
½ pint chicken stock   Large pinch of saffron strands
1 teaspoon good curry powder   Salt and pepper

Set oven to 350°F or Mark 4. Heat the oil in a flameproof casserole dish and brown the lamb shanks all over. Remove the meat and set aside. Add the garlic, ginger and onion and cook for 2 to 3 minutes. Return the lamb to the casserole, stir in the flour and cook for 1 minute. Add the orange juice and rind, the wine and the rice vinegar and cook for 3 to 4 minutes to reduce the sauce. Stir in the stock, saffron and curry powder and season well. Bring back up to heat, cover and transfer to the oven. Cook for about 1½ hours or until the lamb is tender. Serve with boiled rice. Serves 4 to 6.

'Sheep in the Highlands' *by William Watson*

Roast Grouse

The best way to cook a succulent young grouse is to roast it.

Brace of young grouse, plucked and drawn
2 oz butter   2 tablespoons redcurrant jelly
Salt and pepper   6 rashers streaky bacon
2 slices white bread, crusts removed
Giblets   Watercress to garnish

Set oven to 400°F or Mark 6. Rub a little of the butter into the well-washed and dried inside of each bird and spoon the redcurrant jelly into the cavities. Season the outside of the grouse. Cover the breasts with bacon rashers. Place in a roasting tin and cover with kitchen foil. Roast in the oven, allowing 15 minutes per pound weight of 1 bird plus an additional 15 minutes. Meanwhile toast the bread. Put the giblets in saucepan, cover with water and simmer until tender. Strain and reserve the stock to make the gravy. Remove the livers, mash them with butter, salt and pepper and spread on the toast. Slip the toast under each bird for the last 15 minutes of roasting and remove the foil. When cooked, place the grouse and the toast on a serving dish and garnish with watercress. Serve with game chips, redcurrant or rowan jelly and bread sauce. Serves 4.

Game Casserole

Any kind of game can be used for this rich stew with red wine.

6 oz grouse meat
6 oz venison
6 oz hare meat
2 oz diced ham
1 oz seasoned flour
2 oz butter
2 oz onions, chopped
1 oz carrots, chopped
2 oz celery, chopped
¾ pint game stock
3 fl.oz red wine
Salt and pepper

Cut the game meat into cubes and toss in the seasoned flour. Dice the ham. Melt the butter in a heavy bottom casserole dish. Fry the vegetables until soft, then add the game meat and ham and continue frying until browned. Add the game stock and red wine. Bring up to heat, cover with a lid and simmer gently for 1 to 1½ hours, skimming occasionally. Season and serve with mashed potato and redcurrant or rowan jelly. Serves 4 to 6.

'Watering at a Burn' *by John Wright Barker RBA*

Collops of Beef

Collops of beef are traditionally served on Burns Night.

1½ lb piece of braising steak, sliced into 4 collops
2 tablespoons seasoned flour   2 oz butter
1 onion, chopped   6 oz mushrooms, sliced
Bayleaf (optional)   ¾ pint beef stock
Salt and freshly ground black pepper

Set oven to 350°F or Mark 4. Mix the flour with salt and pepper and use to coat the beef slices. Melt the butter in a frying pan. Fry the collops for about 2 minutes on each side, remove from the pan and set aside. Gently fry the onion and the mushrooms. Put the onion and mushrooms and a bayleaf (if desired) into a casserole dish. Lay the collops on top. Pour in the stock and season. Bring up to heat, cover and cook for 1½ hours. Serve with buttered mashed potatoes and a green vegetable. Rowan or redcurrant jelly goes well with this dish. Serves 4.

Hotch Potch

Also known as Hairst Bree (Harvest Broth) this hearty soup probably derives its name from the French work "hochepot", meaning shaken.

1 lb middle neck of lamb, divided into cutlets
2 pints meat stock A bouquet garni Salt and pepper
1 carrot, diced 3 spring onions, finely chopped 1 white turnip, diced
3 oz broad beans 4 oz fresh or frozen peas
½ small cauliflower, broken into florets
½ lettuce ¼ teaspoon finely chopped fresh mint
¼ teaspoon sugar ¼ teaspoon finely chopped fresh parsley

Remove any excess fat from the meat and place in a heavy bottom pan. Add the stock and *bouquet garni* and season. Bring to the boil, cover and simmer for 1 hour, skimming off any scum that rises to the surface. Lift out the meat and remove the flesh from the bones. Skim any fat from the stock and return the meat to the pan. Add the carrot, onions, turnip, broad beans and fresh peas (if using frozen, then these should be added 10 minutes before the end of the cooking time). Cover and simmer for 30 minutes, then add the cauliflower, lettuce, mint and sugar and cook for a further 20 minutes until the vegetables are tender but not breaking up. Remove the *bouquet garni*, check the seasoning and serve garnished with chopped parsley. Serves 4.

Teviotdale Pie

This suet crust pie originates from the Scottish Borders.
It makes a change from Cottage Pie.

1 lb lean beef mince
1 onion, chopped
10 fl.oz beef stock
1 teaspoon Worcestershire sauce
8 oz self raising flour
1 oz cornflour
3 oz shredded beef suet
Milk to mix

Set oven to 350°F or Mark 4. Fry the meat gently over a medium heat until it browns. Add the chopped onion and continue frying until soft. Add the beef stock and Worcestershire sauce and simmer for 15 minutes. Whilst the meat is simmering make the suet crust. Mix the flour, cornflour and suet in a bowl and stir in sufficient milk to produce a thick batter. Put the cooked meat mixture into an ovenproof pie dish, cover with the batter and bake for about 30 minutes until risen and golden. Serves 4.

METRIC CONVERSIONS

The weights, measures and oven temperatures used in the preceding recipes can be easily converted to their metric equivalents. The conversions listed below are only approximate, having been rounded up or down as may be appropriate.

Weights

Avoirdupois	Metric
1 oz.	just under 30 grams
4 oz. (¼ lb.)	app. 115 grams
8 oz. (½ lb.)	app. 230 grams
1 lb.	454 grams

Liquid Measures

Imperial	Metric
1 tablespoon (liquid only)	20 millilitres
1 fl. oz.	app. 30 millilitres
1 gill (¼ pt.)	app. 145 millilitres
½ pt.	app. 285 millilitres
1 pt.	app. 570 millilitres
1 qt.	app. 1.140 litres

Oven Temperatures

	°Fahrenheit	Gas Mark	°Celsius
Slow	300	2	150
	325	3	170
Moderate	350	4	180
	375	5	190
	400	6	200
Hot	425	7	220
	450	8	230
	475	9	240

Flour as specified in these recipes refers to plain flour unless otherwise described.

Acknowledgement: Stacey-Marks Ltd., Fine Art Paintings, Perth.